Quotes & Facts
On
Obama's
Radicalism

**Compiled by
Brian Koralewski**

Contents

Barrack Obama

President of The United States of America

"…I think when you **spread the wealth around,** it's good for everybody."
http://www.nypost.com/p/news/opinion/editorials/item_C0t2Qa7NJlBiD8UAhIrPMI

"**We've got to have a civilian national security force**, that's just as powerful, just as strong, **just as well-funded (as our military)..**
http://www.youtube.com/watch?v=Tt2yGzHfy7s

"There was some suggestion that we might be able to craft something that might meet constitutional muster with respect to caring for fetuses or children who were delivered in this fashion. Unfortunately, this bill goes a little bit further, and so … this is probably not going to survive constitutional scrutiny. Number one, **whenever we define a pre-viable fetus as a person that is protected by the equal protection clause or other elements in the Constitution, what we're really saying is, in fact, that they are persons that are entitled to the kinds of protections that would be provided to a — a child, a nine-month-old — child that was delivered to term.** That determination, then, essentially, if it was accepted by a court, would forbid abortions to take place. I mean, it — it would essentially bar abortions, **because the equal protection clause does not allow somebody to kill a child, and if this is a child,** then this would be an antiabortion statute."

(He is referring to failed partial-birth abortions where the baby is actually born alive. In Illinois, he prevented the Born Alive Infant Protection Act from even having a hearing.) http://www.newsweek.com/2008/08/24/obama-and-infanticide.html

"But (sex education) should also include — it should also include other, you know, information about contraception because, look, I've got two daughters. 9 years old and 6 years old…I am going to teach them first of all about values and morals. But if they make a mistake, **I don't want them punished with a baby.**"

"…**I chose my friends carefully.** The more politically active black students. The foreign students. The Chicanos. The **Marxist Professors** and the structural feminists and punk-rock performance poets. We smoked cigarettes and wore leather jackets. At night, in the dorms, we discussed neocolonialism, Franz Fanon, Eurocentrism, and patriarchy. When we ground out our cigarettes in the hallway carpet or set our stereo soul out and the walls began to shake, we were resisting **bourgeois society's stifling constraints.** "
From "Dreams From My Father," Barrack Obama, p. 101.

"**I happen to be a proponent of a single-payer, universal healthcare plan… A single-payer healthcare plan– universal healthcare plan. That's what I'd like to see**" (2003)

http://www.breitbart.tv/new-obama-claim-i-have-not-said-that-i-was-a-single-payer-supporter/

"Let's say I proposed a plan that **moved to a single-payer system**, let's say- 'Medicare-Plus' – essentially, everybody can buy into Medicare, for example."
http://www.barackobama.com/2007/04/03/obama_visits_portsmouth_for_he.php

"He (President Obama) supports full civil unions and federal rights for LGBT couples and **opposes a constitutional ban on same-sex marriage**…and also believes that **we must ensure adoption rights for all couples and individuals, regardless of their sexual orientation.**"
(http://www.whitehouse.gov/issues/civil_rights/)

"I went to **socialist conferences** at Cooper Union and African cultural fairs in Brooklyn."
(Discussing his time at New York's Columbia University, in the early 80s)
http://www.weeklystandard.com/weblogs/TWSFP/2008/07/is_obama_a_socialist.asp

"But, the Supreme Court never ventured into the issues of **redistribution of wealth** and sort of more basic issues of political and economic justice in this society. And to that extent, **as radical as I think people tried to characterize the Warren Court, it wasn't that radical. It didn't break free from the essential constraints that were placed by the**

founding fathers in the Constitution, as least as it's been interpreted, and Warren Court interpreted in the same way that, generally, the Constitution is a charter of negative liberties, says what the states can't do to you, says what the federal government can't do to you, but it doesn't say what the federal government or the state government must do on your behalf. And that hasn't shifted. **One of the, I think, the tragedies of the civil rights movement, was because the civil rights movement became so court focused, I think that there was a tendency to lose track of the political and community organizing activities on the ground that are able to put together the actual coalitions of power through which you bring about redistributive change,** and in some ways, **we still stuffer from that.**"

(A caller, "Karen," asked if it's "too late for that kind of reparative work economically?" And she asked if that work should be done through the courts or through legislation.)

"Maybe I'm showing my bias here as a legislator as well as a law professor…I'm not optimistic about bringing about **major redistributive change** through the courts. The institution just isn't structured that way."

http://www.cnsnews.com/news/article/38247

"In my view, however, neither approach offers lasting hope of real change for the inner city unless undergirded by a systematic approach to community organization. This is because the issues of the inner city are more complex and deeply rooted than ever before. **Blatant discrimination has been replaced by institutional racism**"

http://illinoisissues.uis.edu/archives/2008/09/whyor
g.html

**"Under my plan of a cap and trade system
electricity rates would necessarily skyrocket,**
even, you know, regardless of what I say about
whether coal is good or bad, because I'm capping
greenhouse gases, coal powered plants, you know,
natural gas, you name it, whatever the plants were,
whatever the industry was, they would have to
retrofit their operations. That will cost money. They
will pass that money on to consumers."
http://www.breitbart.tv/obama-vows-electricity-
rates-would-necessarily-skyrocket-under-his-plan/

"We are five days away from **fundamentally
transforming the United States of America.**"
http://www.realclearpolitics.com/articles/2009/02/th
e_gipper_vs_obama.html

"I think we can say that the **Constitution reflected
an enormous blind spot** in this culture that carries
on until this day, and that **the Framers had that
same blind spot.** I don't think the two views are
contradictory, to say that it was a remarkable
political document that paved the way for where we
are now, and to say that it also reflected **the
fundamental flaw of this country that continues
to this day.**"
http://www.newsmax.com/InsideCover/obama-
constitution/2008/10/27/id/326165

5

"It's not surprising, then, they get bitter, they cling to guns or religion or antipathy to people who aren't like them or anti-immigrant sentiment or anti-trade sentiment as a way to explain their frustrations."
http://www.youtube.com/watch?v=VZWaxjiQyFk&feature=related

Rahm Emanuel

President Obama's Chief of Staff

"Citizenship is not an entitlement program....everyone somewhere between 18 & 25 will serve 3 months of basic training and understanding any kind of basic civil defense...this is not a draft- it's a **universal service...it's required of everybody**"
http://homelessokc.newsvine.com/_news/2009/06/05/2899995-defense-department-establishes-civilian-expeditionary-workforce

"**You never want a serious crisis to go to waste**. And what I mean by that is an opportunity to do things you think you could not do before."
http://www.youtube.com/watch?v=_mzcbXi1Tkk

John Holdren

President Obama's Director of the Office of Science and Technology Policy

When asked recently about his book EcoScience, Holdren said:
"If you read it and you have a problem – you're misreading it."
http://www.breitbart.tv/white-house-science-czar-says-hed-use-free-market-to-de-develop-the-united-states/

"Those who oppose abortion often raise the argument that a decision is being made for an unborn person who 'has no say,'….But unthinking actions of the very same people help to commit future unheard generations to misery and early death on **an overcrowded planet.**"
http://www.cnsnews.com/news/article/51676

"The fetus, given the opportunity to develop properly before birth, and given the essential early socializing experiences and sufficient nourishing food during the crucial **early years after birth, will ultimately develop into a human being,**"
http://www.cnsnews.com/news/article/51676

"The third approach to **population control** is that of involuntary fertility control…**Several coercive proposals deserve discussion mainly because societies may ultimately have to resort to them**

8

unless current trends in birth rates are rapidly reversed by other means."
http://www.washingtonexaminer.com/opinion/blogs/beltway-confidential/Obamas-science-czar-suggested-compulsory-abortion-sterilization-50783612.html

"Indeed, it has been concluded that compulsory population-control laws, **even including laws requiring compulsory abortion, could be sustained under the existing Constitution** if the population crisis became sufficiently severe to endanger the society."
http://www.examiner.com/conservative-politics-in-national/science-czar-john-p-holdren-s-disturbing-beliefs-about-america-capitalism-and-humanity

"It would even be possible to **require** pregnant single women to marry or have **abortions**, perhaps as an alternative to placement for adoption, depending on the society."
http://www.washingtonexaminer.com/opinion/blogs/beltway-confidential/Obamas-science-czar-suggested-compulsory-abortion-sterilization-50783612.html

"**Adding a sterilant to drinking water** or staple foods is a suggestion that seems to horrify people more than most proposals for involuntary fertility control. Indeed, this would pose some very difficult political, legal, and social questions, to say nothing of the technical problems. No such sterilant exists today, nor does one appear to be under

development. To be acceptable, such a substance would have to meet some rather stiff requirements: it must be uniformly effective, despite widely varying doses received by individuals, and despite varying degrees of fertility and sensitivity among individuals; **it must be free of dangerous or unpleasant side effects; and it must have no effect on members of the opposite sex, children, old people, pets, or livestock."**
http://www.examiner.com/conservative-in-sacramento/holdren-science-czar-forced-abortions-mass-sterilizations-planetary-regime-to-save-the-planet?render=print

"Involuntary fertility control: **A program of sterilizing women after their second or third child**, despite the relatively greater difficulty of the operation than vasectomy, might be easier to implement than trying to sterilize men...The development of a long-term sterilizing capsule that could be implanted under the skin and removed when pregnancy is desired opens additional possibilities for coercive fertility control. The capsule could be implanted at puberty and might be removable, **with official permission**, for a limited number of births."
http://www.examiner.com/independent-in-columbia/obama-s-special-advisor-science-czar-john-holdren

"Perhaps those agencies, combined with UNEP and the United Nations population agencies, might eventually be developed into **a Planetary Regime**—sort of an **international superagency for**

population, resources, and environment. Such a comprehensive Planetary Regime could control the development, administration, conservation, and distribution of all natural resources, renewable or nonrenewable, at least insofar as international implications exist. Thus the Regime could have the power to control pollution not only in the atmosphere and oceans, but also in such freshwater bodies as rivers and lakes that cross international boundaries or that discharge into the oceans. The Regime might also be a logical central agency for regulating all international trade, perhaps including assistance from DCs to LDCs, and including all food on the international market."
http://blogs.discovermagazine.com/80beats/2009/04/10/obamas-science-adviser-kicks-up-a-fuss-over-geoengineering/

"**The Planetary Regime might be given responsibility for determining the optimum population for the world and for each region** and for arbitrating various countries' shares within their regional limits. Control of population size might remain the responsibility of each government, but **the Regime would have some power to enforce the agreed limits.**"
http://www.examiner.com/conservative-in-sacramento/holdren-science-czar-forced-abortions-mass-sterilizations-planetary-regime-to-save-the-planet?render=print

"If this could be accomplished, security might be provided by an armed international organization, a global analogue of a police force. Many people

have recognized this as a goal, but the way to reach it remains obscure in a world where factionalism seems, if anything, to be increasing…"
http://www.examiner.com/conservative-in-sacramento/holdren-science-czar-forced-abortions-mass-sterilizations-planetary-regime-to-save-the-planet?render=print

"Individual rights must be balanced against the power of the government to control human reproduction. Some people—respected legislators, judges, and lawyers included—have viewed the right to have children as a fundamental and inalienable right. **Yet neither the Declaration of Independence nor the Constitution mentions a right to reproduce.**" Nor does the UN Charter describe such a right, although a resolution of the United Nations affirms the "right responsibly to choose" the number and spacing of children (emphasis in original). In the United States, individuals have a constitutional right to privacy and it has been held that the right to privacy includes the right to choose whether or not to have children, at least to the extent that a woman has a right to choose not to have children. But the right is not unlimited. Where the society has a "compelling, subordinating interest" in regulating population size, the right of the individual may be curtailed. If society's survival depended on having more children, **women could he required to bear children,** just as men can constitutionally be required to serve in the armed forces.
"Similarly, given a crisis caused by overpopulation, reasonably necessary laws to control excessive reproduction could be enacted. It is often argued

that the right to have children is so personal that the government should not regulate it. In an ideal society, no doubt the state should leave family size and composition solely to the desires of the parents. In today's world, however, the number of children in a family is a matter of profound public concern. The law regulates other highly personal matters. For example, no one may lawfully have more than one spouse at a time. **Why should the law not be able to prevent a person from having more than two children?"**
http://www.wnd.com/?pageId=111475

"210 million now is too many and 280 million in 2040 is likely to be much too many."
http://www.npg.org/notable%20papers/JohnPHoldrenpaper.html

In a 2008 New York Times op-ed, Holdren called climate change skeptics "dangerous."
http://www.nytimes.com/2008/08/04/opinion/04iht-edholdren.1.14991915.html

"The need for de-development presents our economists with a major challenge. They must design a stable, low-consumption economy in which there is a much more equitable distribution of wealth than in the present one. **Redistribution of wealth both within and among nations is absolutely essential**, if a decent life is to be provided for every human being."
http://www.cnsnews.com/news/article/75388

"I think ultimately the rate of growth of material consumption is going to have to come down and there's going to have to be a degree of redistribution of how much we consume in terms of energy and material resources in order to leave room for people who are poor to become more prosperous."
http://www.foxnews.com/story/0,2933,592905,00.ht ml

Ezekiel Emanuel

President Obama's Health Care advisor

"…services provided to individuals who are irreversibly prevented from being or becoming participating citizens are not basic and should not be guaranteed. An obvious example is not guaranteeing health services to patients with dementia. A less obvious example is guaranteeing neuropsychological services to ensure children with learning disabilities can read and learn to reason."
http://www.cnsnews.com/commentary/article/59320

Carol Browner

Assistant to the President, White House Office of Energy & Climate Change

Member of Socialist International (until 2008). She was one of 14 Socialist International leaders of the Commission for a Sustainable World Society.
(Socialist International changed her web mini-bio once she was named to head Obama's energy team.)
http://www.washingtontimes.com/news/2009/jan/12/obama-climate-czar-has-socialist-ties/

Mark Lloyd

President Obama's FCC Associate General Counsel and Chief Diversity Officer

Proposed fining conservative radio stations up to $250 Million and giving proceeds to government-subsidized Corporation for Public Broadcasting. http://www.wnd.com/?pageId=106808

"It should be clear by now that my focus here is not freedom of speech or the press….This freedom is too often an exaggeration….At the very least, blind references to freedom of speech or the press serve as a distraction from the critical examination of other communications policies." http://www.cnsnews.com/news/article/55420

"…simply reinstating **the Fairness Doctrine** will do little to address the gap between conservative and progressive talk unless the underlying elements of the public trustee doctrine are enforced, in particular, the requirements of local accountability and the reasonable airing of important matters." http://www.religionnews.com/index.php?/rnstext/fairness_doctrine_still_dead_but_groups_still_worried/

"In **Venezuela with Chavez, really an incredible revolution**- a dramatic revolution – to begin to put in place, saying that "we're going to have impact on the people of Venezuela"….the property owners and the folks who were then controlling the media in Venezuela rebelled- work(ed), frankly with folks here in the U.S. Government, worked to oust him….. and (he- Chavez) came back and had another revolution. And **Chavez then started to take the media very seriously in this country."** http://blogs.abcnews.com/politicalpunch/2009/08/o bama-dont-let-public-option-debate-overshadow-reform.html

"The problem of media bias is as you know not simply a matter of taste, it is a problem of life and death, of war, of peace. Solving our problems, we're descending into confusion. **There is no greater or more urgent problem facing America today…."** http://www.americanprogress.org/issues/2005/06/b8 16321.html

"There are few things I think more frightening in the American mind than dark skin black men. Here I am." http://www.breitbart.tv/fcc-%E2%80%98diversity-czar%E2%80%99-few-things-frighten-americans-more-than-%E2%80%98dark-skin-black-men%E2%80%99/

"(Diversity requires asking) **who is going to step down (so) someone else can have power?"** http://newsbusters.org/blogs/seton-motley/2009/09/23/fccs-diversity-czar-white-people-need-be-forced-step-down-so-someone-0

"What we are really saying is **the Fairness Doctrine is not enough…unless you put some teeth into that**...with some hard, structural rules in place that are going to result in fairness."
http://toledotalk.com/cgi-bin/tt.pl/article/43894

Edward Said

The Said-Khalidi-Obama Connection
Edward Said hated Israel so much that he was seen throwing rocks from Lebanon at Israeli soldiers across the border.
Andrew McCarthy said: "Obama was a student at Columbia from 1981 to 1983. He refuses to discuss those years; it is known only that he studied for at least some time under Edward Said, the late PLO apologist."
http://www.freerepublic.com/focus/f-news/2113848/posts
http://www.regularfolksunited.com/index.php?tab=article_view&article_id=2547

Kevin Jennings

President Obama's Safe Schools Advisor

Wrote the foreword for a book titled: **"Queering of Elementary Education."** (Another foreword was written for the same book by William Ayers, an unrepentant terrorist.)
http://www.cnsnews.com/news/article/56196

Praised Harry Hay as somebody who inspired him. Harry Hay associated with the group NAMBLA (North American **Man/Boy Love Association**) & was a pioneer in the gay civil rights movement.
http://www.washingtonexaminer.com/opinion/blogs/beltway-confidential/Obama-appointee-lauded-NAMBLA-figure-63115112.html

"I can envision a day when straight people say, 'So what if you're promoting homosexuality?'… That is our mission from this day forward."
http://blackchristiannews.com/news/2009/10/obamas-safe-schools-czar-backs-gay-curriculum.html

Harold Koh

President Obama's pick for State Department's legal adviser

"I'd rather have [former Supreme Court Justice Harry] Blackmun, who uses the wrong reasoning in Roe [v. Wade] **to get the right results, and let other people figure out the right reasoning.**"
http://www.nypost.com/p/news/opinion/opedcolum
nists/item_yyMKJnrmyV5g5MZlhheZOP;jsessioni
d=ABA3B3841BBDA198B82E3E39129B951E

"What role can transnational legal process play in affecting the behavior of several nations whose disobedience with international law has attracted global attention after September 11th — most prominently, **North Korea, Iraq and our own country, the United States of America**? For shorthand purposes, **I will call these countries 'the axis of disobedience.'**"
http://www.washingtontimes.com/news/2009/oct/14
/undermining-honduras/

Kenneth Feinberg

Special Master for TARP Executive Compensation

"The statute provides these guideposts, but the statute ultimately says **I have discretion to decide what it is that these people should make** and that my determination will be final… **Anything is possible under the law.**"
http://townhall.com/columnists/MichelleMalkin/2009/08/19/the_pay_czars_power_grab

Cass Sunstein

President Obama's close friend
&
Director of the Office of Information and
Regulatory Affairs

"We ought to **ban hunting.**"
http://www.consumerfreedom.com/news_detail.cfm
/h/3807-exposed-the-secret-animal-rights-agenda-
of-americas-next-regulatory-czar

**"Almost all gun control legislation is
constitutionally fine.** And if the Court is right,
then **fundamentalism does not justify the view
that the Second Amendment protects an
individual right to bear arms."**
http://www.foxnews.com/story/0,2933,570562,00.ht
ml

"Animals should be permitted to bring suit, with
human beings as their representatives ..."
"Animal rights: current debates and new
directions," by Cass R. Sunstein, Martha Craven
Nussbaum, p. 249

**"[Humans'] willingness to subject animals to
unjustified suffering** will be seen ... as a form of
unconscionable barbarity...**morally akin to slavery
and the mass extermination of human beings."**
(2007 speech at Harvard University)

24

"A system of limitless individual choices, with respect to communications, is not necessarily in the interest of citizenship and self-government."
"Republic.com 2.0," by Cass Sunstein, p. 137

"Consider **the view that the Second Amendment confers an individual right to own guns.** The view is respectable, but **it may be wrong**, and prominent specialists reject it on various grounds. As late as 1980, it would have been preposterous to argue that the Second Amendment creates an individual right to own guns, and no federal court invalidated a gun control restriction on Second Amendment grounds until 2007. Yet countless Americans politicians, in recent years, have acknowledged that they respect the individual right to bear arms, at least in general terms. Their views are a product of the energetic efforts of meaning entrepreneurs – some from the National Rifle Association, who have press a particular view of the Second Amendment."
Cass R. Sunstein, *A Constitution of Many Minds*, Princeton University Press, 2009, p. 172-173

"The National Association of Broadcasters and others with similar economic interests typically use the First Amendment in precisely the same way the National Rifle Association uses the Second Amendment. We should think of the two camps as

jurisprudential twins. The National Association of Broadcasters is prepared to make self-serving and outlandish claims about the First Amendment before the public and before the courts, and to pay lawyers and publicists a lot of money to help establish those claims.(Perhaps they will ultimately succeed.) The National Rifle Association does the same thing with the Second Amendment. In both cases, those whose social and economic interests are at stake are prepared to use the Constitution, however implausibly invoked, in order to give a veneer of principle and respectability to arguments that would otherwise seem hopelessly partisan and self-interested."
"Republic.com 2.0," by Cass Sunstein, p. 173

"The Second Amendment seems to specify its own purpose, which is to protect the "well regulated Militia." If that is the purpose of the Second Amendment (as Burger believed), then we might speculate that it safeguards not individual rights but federalism"
http://www.powells.com/blog/?p=2627

"Those who emphasize suffering have a simple answer to this objection: Everything depends on whether and to what extent the animal in question is capable of suffering. **If rats are able to suffer, then their interests are relevant to the question of how, and perhaps even whether, they can be expelled from houses.**"
"Animal rights: current debates and new directions," by Cass R. Sunstein, Martha Craven Nussbaum, p. 12

"I have argued in favor of a reformulation of First Amendment law. The overriding goal of the reformulation is to reinvigorate processes of democratic deliberation, by ensuring greater attention to public issues and greater diversity of views. **The First Amendment should not stand as an obstacle to democratic efforts to accomplish these goals.** A New Deal for speech would draw on Justice Brandeis' insistence on the role of free speech in promoting political deliberation and citizenship. It would reject Justice Holmes' "marketplace" conception of free speech, a conception that disserves the aspirations of those who wrote America's founding document."
Cass R. Sunstein, *Democracy and the Problem of Free Speech,* The Free Press,
1995, p. 119

"Consider the "fairness doctrine," now largely abandoned but once requiring radio and television broadcasters:
'...[I]n light of astonishing economic and technological changes, **we must doubt whether, as interpreted, the constitutional guarantee of free speech is adequately serving democratic goals. It is past time for a large-scale reassessment of the appropriate role of the First Amendment in the democratic process.'"**
Cass R. Sunstein, *Democracy and the Problem of Free Speech,* The Free Press,
1995, p. xi

"In what sense in the money in our pockets and bank accounts fully 'ours'? Did we earn it by our own autonomous efforts? Could we have inherited it without the assistance of probate courts? Do we save it without the support of bank regulators? Could we spend it if there were no public officials to coordinate the efforts and pool the resources of the community in which we live?… Without taxes there would be no liberty. Without taxes there would be no property. Without taxes, few of us would have any assets worth defending. [It is] a dim fiction that some people enjoy and exercise their rights without placing any burden whatsoever on the public fisc. … There is no liberty without dependency. **That is why we should celebrate tax day …**"
Cass R. Sunstein, "Why We Should Celebrate Paying Taxes," *The Chicago Tribune,* April 14, 1999

"My major aim in this book is to uncover **an important but neglected part of America's heritage: the idea of a second bill of rights.** In brief, the second bill attempts to protect both opportunity and security, by **creating rights to employment,** adequate food and clothing, decent shelter, education, recreation, and medical care."
Cass R. Sunstein, *The Second Bill of Rights: FDR's Unfinished Revolution and Why We Need it More Than Ever*, Basic Books, New York, 2004, p. 1

"Much of the time, the United States seems to have embraced **a confused and pernicious form of**

individualism. This approach endorses rights of private property and freedom of contract, and respects political liberty, but claims to distrust "government intervention" and insists that people must fend for themselves. This form of so-called individualism is incoherent, a tangle of confusions." Cass R. Sunstein, *The Second Bill of Rights: FDR's Unfinished Revolution and Why We Need it More Than Ever*, Basic Books, New York, 2004, p. 3

"It is even possible that **desirable redistribution is more likely to occur through climate change policy than otherwise**...or to be accomplished more effectively through climate policy than through direct foreign aid."
http://www.wnd.com/?pageId=112243

Van Jones

Special Advisor for Green Jobs, Enterprise and Innovation in the White House

In 1994, helped form a **socialist** collective, Standing Together to Organize a **Revolutionary** Movement (STORM) which **held study groups on the theories of Marx and Lenin and dreamed of a multiracial socialist utopia.** They protested police brutality and **got arrested for crashing through police barricades..**
http://www.foxnews.com/politics/2009/09/03/raw-data-van-jones-resume/
http://www.gfn.org/kristen/category/wordpress-tag/van-jones-glenn-beck

Jones signed a statement for 911Truth.org in 2004 demanding an investigation into what the Bush Administration may have done that "deliberately allowed 9/11 to happen, perhaps as a pretext for war."
http://www.washingtontimes.com/weblogs/back-story/2009/sep/03/green-jobs-czar-signed-truther-statement-in-2004/

"I was a rowdy nationalist on April 28th [1992], and then the verdicts came down on April 29th. By August, **I was a communist.**"
http://www.wnd.com/?pageId=108445

"I met all these young radical people of color – I mean **really radical: communists and anarchists. And it was, like, 'This is what I need to be a part of.' I spent the next ten years of my life working with a lot of those people I met in jail, trying to be a revolutionary."**
http://newzeal.blogspot.com/2009/04/obama-file-72-obama-appoints-former.html

Leading member of STORM, which described itself as having a **"commitment to the fundamental ideas of Marxism-Leninism."**
http://www.wnd.com/?pageId=108445

'**We agreed with Lenin's analysis of the state** and the party,' reads the manifesto. '**And we found inspiration in the revolutionary strategies developed by Third World revolutionaries like Mao Tse-tung** and Amilcar Cabral.' Cabral is the late Marxist revolutionary leader of Guinea-Bissau and the Cape Verde Islands. **WND previously reported Jones named his son after Cabral and reportedly concludes every e-mail with a quote from the communist leader.**
http://www.ednews.org/articles/white-house-rowdy-communist-held-vigil-for-muslims.html

"I'm willing to forego the cheap satisfaction of the radical pose for the deep satisfaction of the **radical ends."**
When asked if he is a Marxist -in Feb. '09.
http://www.youtube.com/watch?v=dJAfHySClWA

31

"How is that capitalism working for you? How is that capitalism working for you? How is that capitalism working for you this year?…This movement is deeper than a solar panel, deeper than a solar panel. Don't stop there. Don't stop there. No, we're going to change the whole system. We're going to change the whole thing….In this stage of the struggle, and I'll only speak to this stage of the struggle, I'm the best ….capitalist ever had. Thank you very much. …And this won't we have to prepare for this to be a long process even though it probably won't be. We have to prepare ourselves. We can't just push the people…We have to listen, listen, listen, listen. And then learn. And then co lead, try to coauthor a different future with folks. And we have to assume that's going to take a long time, but sometimes what should have taken another 20 years, Barack Hussein Obama, can take a season…..And this won't we have to prepare for this to be a long process even though it probably won't be."
http://www.glennbeck.com/content/articles/article/198/30037/

"What about our immigrant sisters and brothers? What about our immigrant sisters and brothers? What about people who come here from all around the world who we're willing to have out in the field, with poison being sprayed on them, poison being sprayed on them because we have the wrong agricultural system. And we're willing to poison them and poison the earth to put food on our table, but we don't want to give them rights and we don't

32

want to give them dignity and we don't want to give them respect?"
http://www.tnr.com/blog/the-spine/cool-yes-communist

"The white polluters and the white environmentalists are essentially steering poison into the people of color communities."
http://www.foxnews.com/politics/2009/09/03/raw-data-van-jones-words/

"You've never seen a Columbine done by a black child. Never. They always say we can't believe it happened here. We can't believe it's these — suburban white kids. It's only them."
http://www.breitbart.tv/van-jones-only-suburbal-white-kids-shoot-up-schools/

"And our Native American sisters and brothers who were pushed and bullied and mistreated and shoved into all the land we didn't want, where it was all hot and windy. Well, guess what? Renewable energy? Guess what, solar industry? Guess what wind industry? They now own and control 80 percent of the renewable energy resources. No more broken treaties. No more broken treaties. **Give them the wealth! Give them the wealth!** Give them the dignity. Give them the respect that they deserve. No justice on stolen land. We owe them a debt."
http://www.youtube.com/watch?v=Uu63VWh8Pdg

"Right after Rosa Parks refused to give up her seat if the civil rights leaders had jumped out and said, 'OK now we want reparations for slavery, **we want redistribution of all the wealth,** and we want to legalize mixed marriages.' If we'd come out with a maximum program the very next day, they'd been laughed at. Instead they came out with a very minimum. 'We just want to integrate these buses.' But, inside that minimum demand was **a very radical kernel that eventually meant that from 1964 to 1968 complete revolution was on the table** for this country. And, I think that this green movement has to pursue those same steps and stages. Right now we say we want to move from suicidal gray capitalism to something eco-capitalism where at least we're not fast-tracking the destruction of the whole planet. Will that be enough? No, it won't be enough. We want to go beyond the systems of exploitation and oppression altogether. But, that's a process and I think that's what's great about the movement that is beginning to emerge is that the crisis is so severe in terms of joblessness, violence and now ecological threats that people are willing to be both pragmatic and visionary. So the green economy will start off as a small subset and **we are going to push it and push it and push it until it becomes the engine for transforming the whole society.**"
http://www.wnd.com/?pageId=126667

34

Valerie Jarrett

President Obama's Senior Adviser

"**Van Jones, we were so delighted to be able to recruit him into the White House. We've been watching him, really, for — it's not that over — for as long as he has been active out in Oakland** and all of the ways that he has — creative ideas that he has. And so now we have captured that and we have all of that energy and enthusiasm in the White House."
http://www.foxnews.com/story/0,2933,548381,00.html

Anita Dunn

President Obama's White House Communications Director

"And then the third lesson and tip actually come from two of **my favorite political philosophers, Mao Tse-tung** and Mother Teresa — not often coupled with each together, but the two people that I turn to most to basically deliver a simple point, which is, you're going to make choices. You're going to challenge. You're going to say, 'Why not?' You're going to figure out how to do things that have never been done before. But here's the deal: These are your choices. They are no one else's. In 1947, when Mao Tse-tung was being challenged within his own party on his plan to basically take China over, Chiang Kai-shek and the Nationalist Chinese held the cities, they had the army, they had the air force, they had everything on their side. And people said, 'How can you win? How can you do this? How can you do this against all of the odds against you?' And Mao Zedong said, you know, 'You fight your war, and I'll fight mine.'"
http://www.cnsnews.com/news/article/55665

(A quick primer on Mao Tse-tung: "Mao's responsibility for the extinction of anywhere from 40 to 70 million lives brands him as a mass killer greater than Hitler or Stalin, his indifference to the suffering and the loss of humans breathtaking." Fenby, Jonathan. Modern China: The Fall and Rise of a Great Power, 1850 to the Present. Ecco, 2008. ISBN 0-06-166116-3 p. 351)

"Very rarely did we communicate through the press anything that we didn't absolutely control…One of the reasons we did so many of the David Plouffe (Obama's chief campaign manager) videos was not just for our supporters, but also because it was a way for us to get our message out without having to actually talk to reporters…We just put that out there and made them write what Plouffe had said as opposed to Plouffe doing an interview with a reporter. So it was very much we controlled it as opposed to the press controlled it…Whether it was a David Plouffe video or an Obama speech, a huge part of our press strategy was focused on making the media cover what Obama was actually saying **as opposed to why the campaign was saying it, what the tactic was**…Making the press cover what we were saying."

http://www.youtube.com/watch?v=TLR5jHlytRg

Jerry Kellman

In 1985, freshly graduated from Columbia University and working for a New York business consultant, Barack Obama decided to become a community organizer. He got a call from Jerry Kellman, an organizer working on Chicago's far South Side...Kellman was looking for an organizer for the new Developing Communities Project (DCP), which would focus on black city neighborhoods...**Obama moved to Chicago to be part of the Jerry Kellman organization as a community organizer...Kellman was a Saul Alinsky protégé...Among the primary goals of Saul Alinsky, author of "Rules for Radicals"** (and known as the "father of modern American radicalism"), **was radical socialism and redistribution of wealth. Alinsky taught his protégés to "hide" their true goals by any means necessary. Lying was fine.** The objective of Alinsky and Kellman was to turn people against the white establishment.
http://www.riehlworldview.com/carnivorous_conservative/2008/08/michelle-os-ali.html

38

David Axelrod

President Obama's White House Senior Adviser

Axelrod wrote a raving review of the book, "Listen to Your Mother: Stand Up Straight- How Progressives Can Win," calling it a "blueprint" for future progressive victories.
This book was written by Robert Creamer, who was in prison at the time for stealing $2 million from banks through check fraud. Robert Creamer was convicted of that felony and thrown in prison where he wrote this book. On the acknowledgement page, he praises Saul Alinsky as the "legendary community organizer."
http://www.discoverthenetworks.org/individualProfile.asp?indid=2438

Roughly, here are the points Creamer makes and how they apply to a health takeover:
Must declare health insurance a right of all Americans and government must provide it.
Must create a belief that health care is in crisis.
Must create messages depicting private health insurance as a failure.
Must form relationships with the business community (such as big pharma, AMA, AARP, Hospital Associations)
Must convince political leaders they risk their careers if they don't support health care program.
Must foster a process that can ultimately yield consensus. (National Endowment for the Arts urges Hollywood to script TV and movies backing health plan).

Must organize a national field program (SEIU, ACORN, MOVEON, AARP) to bring the program to neighborhoods.
Must focus on mobilizing Churches and the labor movement for health program.
Must leverage connections and resources of all private, public, union, religious groups in order to pass health care and bring about redistributive change.
Must raise ample amount of money to assure that all is permanently put into place.
The book urges its progressive followers to raise the emotions of fear, anger, disgust and revulsion throughout America to get the change and usurp the power.
http://www.cdobs.com/archive/featured/a-felon-at-the-white-house-how-much-influence-does-bob-creamer-have/

Manning Marable

"**Obama represents** a generation of what might be called post-racial black politicians-by which I mean they espouse a politics that minimizes matters of race. **They do not like to talk about race and subsume it under the rubric of poverty and class.** So they are generally left of centre, or liberal, on social and economic policy. Obama is a progressive liberal…**What makes Obama different** is that he has also been a community organizer. He has read left literature, including my works, and **he understands what socialism is. A lot of the people working with him are, indeed, socialists with backgrounds in the Communist Party or as independent Marxists.** There are a lot of people like that in Chicago who have worked with him for years…"
http://newzeal.blogspot.com/2009/01/obama-file-62-obama-understands-what.html

John L. McKnight

In the early to mid-1980s, McKnight helped train Barack Obama in the agitation/**infiltration tactics of Alinsky,** whose 'Reveille for **Radicals'** has been a blueprint for the revolutionary activism of "community organizers" since its 1946 publication, as has Alinsky's 1972 book 'Rules for **Radicals.' From McKnight and other expositors of the Alinsky method, Obama today claims to have received the "best education I ever had, better than anything I got at Harvard Law School."**
http://www.nytimes.com/2008/07/07/us/politics/07community.html

Saul Alinsky dedicated the first edition of his book, "Rules for Radicals," to Satan: "Lest we forget at least an over-the-shoulder acknowledgment to the very first radical known to man who rebelled against the establishment and did it so effectively that he at least won his own kingdom – Lucifer."
http://www.wnd.com/?pageId=76170

Frank Marshall Davis

Father-figure to President Obama

Member of Communist Party USA (CPUSA) (In the 1951 report of the Commission on Subversive Activities to the Legislature of the Territory of Hawaii) The CPUSA had tens of thousands of members, some of them covert agents who had penetrated the U.S. Government. It received secret subsidies from the old Soviet Union. **There was a 601 page FBI file on him. Was a mentor to Obama from age 10-18.**
http://www.freerepublic.com/focus/bloggers/2107234/posts

Obama, in his book, "Dreams From My Father," refers to him repeatedly as "Frank." and says Davis called college "An advanced degree in compromise" and warned Obama not to forget his "people" and not to "start believing what they tell you about equal opportunity and the American way and all that ####."
"Dreams from My Father: A Story of Race and Inheritance," by Barack Obama, p. 97

Sonia Sotomayor

President Obama's Nominee for the Supreme Court

"I would hope that a wise **Latina woman** with the richness of her experiences would more often than not reach **a better conclusion than a white male** who hasn't lived that life."
http://www.nytimes.com/2009/05/15/us/15judge.html

"**Court of Appeals is where policy is made**…and I know this is on tape and I should never say this, because we don't make law I know…"
http://abcnews.go.com/Politics/SoniaSotomayor/story?id=7685284

Sotomayor, self-admittedly claimed that it is a judges job to make policy, rather than adjudicate and interpret constitutional law….This…should prevent her from being a judge at all, much less a Supreme Court justice. **She has been overturned 80% (4 out of 5 times) by the Supreme Court when they reviewed opinions that she authored.**3 out of the 4 times the Court held that Judge Sotomayor erred in her statutory interpretation.
http://silentnomoremajority.newsvine.com/_news/2009/06/01/2884854-sonia-sotomayors-quotes-reveal-complete-ignorance-on-the-duties-of-our-judicial-branch-
&
http://www.sendemallhome.com/2009/07/sotomayor-update-new-haven-decision.html

"…I wonder whether by **ignoring** our differences as women or men of **color we do a disservice** both to the law and society."
http://www.nytimes.com/2009/05/15/us/politics/15judge.text.html?pagewanted=4

Robert Reich

President Obama's Economic advisor

"I will actually give you a speech…of what a candidate for president would say if that candidate did not care about becoming president. In other words, this **is what the truth is and a candidate will never say, but what candidates should say if we were in a kind of democracy where citizens were honored**….Let me tell you a few things on healthcare. Look, we are we have the only healthcare system in the world that is designed to avoid sick people. That's true. And what I'm going to do is I am going to try to reorganize it to be more amenable to treating sick people, but that means you. Particularly you young people. Particularly you **young, healthy people- you are going to have to pay more.** And by the way, we are going to have to, **if you are very old- we're not going to give you all that technology and all those drugs for the last couple of years of your life** to keep you maybe going for another couple of months. **It's too expensive. So we're going to let you die."**
http://online.wsj.com/article/SB1000142405274870
4107204574473331382043514.html

Bernie Sanders

Obama campaigned for this self-avowed socialist.
http://www.youtube.com/watch?v=tIlIpOkRh2A

President **Obama was ranked the most liberal senator , even more liberal than self-avowed socialist Bernie Sanders:**
http://nj.nationaljournal.com/voteratings/sen/lib_co ns.htm?o1=lib_composite&o2=desc#results

Jeremiah Wright

President Obama's pastor for the 20 years immediately preceding his presidency

http://www.nytimes.com/2008/06/01/us/politics/01o
bama.html?_r=1&bl&ex=1212552000&en=4f275b
18627314ec&ei=5087%0A

Obama said about Wright: "Did I know him
(Jeremiah Wright) to be an occasionally fierce critic
of American domestic and foreign policy? Of
course."
http://www.nationalreview.com/campaign-
spot/9739/obamas-philadelphia-speech-looks-
ridiculous-now

Wright said about Obama: "When Obama threw
me under the bus, he threw me under the bus
literally!"
http://content.usatoday.com/communities/ondeadlin
e/post/2010/05/rev-wright-says-obama-threw-me-
under-the-bus/1

Obama also said about Wright: **"Did I ever hear
him (Jeremiah Wright) make remarks that
would be considered controversial while I sat in
the church? Yes."**
http://www.foxnews.com/story/0,2933,553880,00.ht
ml

Obama also said about Wright's church on a separate occasion: **"I don't think my church is actually particularly controversial."** http://abcnews.go.com/Blotter/DemocraticDebate/story?id=4443788&page=1

Quotes by Wright:

"The government gives them the drugs, builds bigger prisons, passes a three-strike law, and then wants us to sing God Bless America? No, no, no! Not God bless America. **God damn America!** It's in the Bible, for killing innocent people. **God damn America** for treating its citizens as less than human!" http://www.youtube.com/watch?v=nH5ixmT83JE

"And they will not only attack you if you try to point out what's going on in white America, **the U.S. of KKK A.**" http://www.youtube.com/watch?v=DGiNtj-0m0A

"We bombed Hiroshima, we bombed Nagasaki, and **we nuked far more than the thousands in New York and the Pentagon and we never batted an eye.** We have supported state terrorism against the Palestinians and black South Africans, and now we are indignant?! Because the stuff we have done overseas is not brought back into our front yard? **Americans chickens are coming home to roost.**" http://www.youtube.com/watch?v=36T1fnIafC0

"The government lied about inventing the HIV virus as a means of genocide against people of color. The government lied."
http://www.wnd.com/?pageId=58928

"Barack knows what it means living in a country and a culture that is controlled by rich white people....Hillary would never know that. Hillary ain't never been called a nigger. Hillary has never had a people defined as a non-person."
http://www.nationalreview.com/articles/223926/wright-and-wrong/kathryn-jean-lopez

"Grateful for the opportunity to bring you a word of Thanksgiving from those who don't ordinarily get a hearing unless they go along with the program, sing in tune with whatever is the popular tune and stay in lockstep with the political pundits who tell us what is politically correct, what is permissible and what will be tolerated from a person of color in this land, the land of the greed and the home of the brave excuse me, the land of the greed and home of the slave...My work with liberation theology, with Latin American theologians, with the Black Theology Project and what the Cuban Council of Churches taught me 30 years ago the importance of Marx and the Marxist analysis of the sociologies of the vulnerable and the oppressed who were trying desperately to break free of the political economies undergirded by this country that were choking them and cutting off any hope of a possible future where all of the people would benefit."

(Speech at the anniversary celebration of the Socialist magazine *Monthly Review)*
http://www.glennbeck.com/content/articles/article/198/32661/

Michelle Obama

1st Lady – President Obama's Wife

"For the **first time** in my adult life, I am **proud of my country…**"
http://www.breitbart.tv/michelle-obama-first-time-in-my-adult-lifetime-i-am-really-proud-of-my-country/

"Barack stood up that day (talking about a visit to Chicago neighborhoods), and spoke words that have stayed with me ever since. He talked about **'The world as it is' and 'The world as it should be…'**…All of us driven by a simple belief that **the world as it is** just won't do – that we have an obligation to **fight for the world as it should be.**"
http://www.wnd.com/?pageId=73533

(Compare this quote with quote from Saul Alinsky's book, "Rules for Radicals:"
"The means-and-ends moralists, constantly obsessed with the ethics of the means used by the Have-Nots against the Haves, should search themselves as to their real political position. In fact, they are passive — but real — allies of the Haves…The most unethical of all means is the non-use of any means… The standards of judgment must be rooted in the whys and wherefores of life as it is lived, **the world as it is, not our wished-for fantasy of the world as it should be.**"
http://www.crossroad.to/Quotes/communism/alinsky.htm

And this one too:

"What follows is **for those who want to change the world from what it is to what they believe it should be.** 'The Prince' was written by Machiavelli for the Haves on how to hold power. 'Rules for Radicals' is written for the Have-Nots on how to take it away. In this book **we are concerned with how to create mass organizations to seize power and give it to the people;** to realize the democratic dream of equality, justice, peace, co-operation, equal and full opportunities for education, full and useful employment, health…We are talking about a mass power organization which will change the world…This means revolution."
http://www.crossroad.to/Quotes/communism/alinsky.htm

"The truth is most Americans don't want much. Folks don't want the whole pie. Most Americans feel blessed to thrive a little bit, but that's out of reach for them. The truth is, in order to get things like universal health care and a revamped education system, someone is going to have to give up a piece of their pie so that someone else can have more."

William Ayers

Close associate & supporter of the President

Former leader of the Weather Underground,
a radical left organization in the 1970s that bombed
the U.S. Capitol And the Pentagon during that time.
http://www.nytimes.com/2008/10/04/us/politics/04a
yers.html
and
Russell Berman, "Obama's Ties To Left Come
Under Scrutiny," The New York Sun, 2/19/08

"The link given below is an image of a newspaper
clipping that shows a review of Ayer's book by
Barrack Obama.
http://www.zombietime.com/zomblog/?p=64

Ayers visited the White House twice in 2009.
http://www.washingtonpost.com/wp-
dyn/content/article/2009/10/30/AR2009103003735.
html

Obama's career was launched at Ayers' home.
http://articles.latimes.com/2008/apr/18/nation/na-
radicals18

"I don't regret setting bombs. I feel we didn't do
enough."

http://query.nytimes.com/gst/fullpage.html?res=9F0
2E1DE1438F932A2575AC0A9679C8B63&sec=&s
pon=&pagewanted=all

Here are some other facts:

Ayers' Wife And Fellow Weather Underground
Leader, Bernadine Dohrn, Appeared On The FBI's
Most Wanted List Prior To Her Surrender To
Authorities In 1980.
James Litke, "Fugitive Leader Surrenders With No
Regrets," The Associated Press, 12/4/80

Ayers And Other Leaders Of The Weather
Underground Set Up A Bomb Factory In New
York, Planning To Blow Up Ft. Dix In New Jersey
And Various Police Headquarters.
Jon Anderson, "Weathering Change '60s
Revolutionary Bill Ayers Says He Has Always
Been A Teacher, But He No Longer Uses Bombs
As Study Aids," Chicago Tribune, 7/8/93

The Bomb Factory Accidentally Exploded In 1970,
Leveling The Townhouse And Killing Three
People.
(ibid)

In 1969, Ayers And 300 Other Radicals Launched
An Unsuccessful Attack On The Home Of U.S.
District Judge Julius Hoffman.
(ibid)

Ayers Is "Flatly Unrepentant About The Bombings."
Ben Smith, "Obama Once Visited '60s Radicals," The Politico, 2/22/08

George Soros

4 visits to the White House in 2009
http://www.politico.com/news/stories/1009/28950.html

CNSNews.com reports that, "Not only did Soros donate to Obama's campaign, but four other family members – Jennifer, sons Jonathan and Robert and wife Susan – did as well. Because of a special provision campaign finance laws, the Soroses were able to give a collective $60,000 to Obama during his primary challenge."
http://federalism.typepad.com/crime_federalism/2009/08/barack-obama-gives-kicback-to-george-soros.html

"No, I think this would be the time because you really need to bring China into the creation of a **new world order, financial world order**."
http://bighollywood.breitbart.com/mvadum/2010/10/21/soros-funded-documentary-embraces-left-wing-terrorists-who-plotted-to-kill-republicans/

Andy Stern

22 Visits to the White House in 2009

President of the Service Employees International Union (SEIU)
http://blogs.wsj.com/washwire/2009/10/30/seius-stern-tops-white-house-visitor-list/

"And we are beginning, we have offices now in Australia and in Switzerland, in London, in South America, in Africa. We've been working with unions around the world. And what we're working towards is **building a global organization** because **workers of the world unite. It's not just a slogan anymore. It's a way we're going to have to do our work…We're trying to use the power of persuasion. And if that doesn't work, we'll use the persuasion of power** because there are governments and there are opportunities to change laws that effect these companies. I'm not naive. We're ready to strike… (reporter asked: 'It started last summer with the so called big box. Labor wanted it; business didn't.') **We took names. We watched how they voted. We know where they live.** There are opportunities in America to **share better in the wealth, to rebalance the power, and unions and government are part of the solution.**"
http://www.youtube.com/watch?v=xSllsTLkBsw

John Podesta

17 visits to the White House in 2009.
http://www.foxnews.com/politics/2009/10/31/celebs-lobbyists-white-house-guests/

Co-chairman of the Obama-Biden Transition Project
http://en.wikipedia.org/wiki/Presidential_transition_of_Barack_Obama

Podesta's most lasting contribution to the leftist cause came through his promotion of a strategy that White House aides dubbed "Project Podesta." This was a system that enabled the Clintons to push through unpopular policies that neither Congress nor the American people wanted. Its implementation marked a dramatic tilt in the balance of power, giving the executive branch an unprecedented ability to force its will on the legislative branch. Project Podesta enabled the President to bypass Congress through the use of executive orders, presidential decision directives, White-House-sponsored lawsuits, vacancy appointments to high federal office, selective regulatory actions against targeted corporations, and a host of other extra-constitutional tactics.
http://www.rules.house.gov/archives/rules_tran08.htm

Podesta was appointed President and CEO of the Center for American Progress (CAP) at its founding on July 7, 2003. He was hand-picked for the job by CAP founders George Soros and Morton H. Halperin

http://www.americanprogress.org/experts/PodestaJohn.html

http://www.freerepublic.com/focus/f-news/2128986/posts

"Van Jones is an exceptional and inspired leader who has fought to bring economic and environmental justice to communities across our country."

http://www.aim.org/aim-column/a-socialist-on-the-high-court-part-two/

Ron Bloom

President Obama's Senior Advisor for Manufacturing

"Generally speaking we get the joke. We know that **the free market is nonsense**. We know that the whole point is to game the system, to beat the market, or at least find someone who will pay you a lot of money because they're convinced that there is a free lunch. We know this is largely about power, that it's an adults only, no limit game. We kind of agree with Mao that political power comes largely from the barrel of a gun. And we get it that if you want a friend, you should get a dog."
http://www.youtube.com/watch?v=ykENW-l91SA

Jim Wallis

Obama's Spiritual Advisor

"We've (Obama & I have) been talking faith and politics for a long time."
http://archive.frontpagemag.com/readArticle.aspx?ARTID=34385

"My Dorothy Day story happened in Chicago. She was just leaving as we were coming on the scene. So we were living in Chicago. So I ran 20 blocks. And in the parlor of the Catholic Worker— and in walks the great lady. Dorothy wrote a book about her life called "Love is the Measure." But she wasn't ever soft. Very tough. So you're a radical student like me, right? You're a Marxist like me, right?'
(I said) 'Yeah'"
http://www.breitbart.tv/obama-advisor-jim-wallis-explores-wealth-marxism-social-justice/
http://www.discoverthenetworks.org/individualProfile.asp?indid=1833(background of Wallis' open activism for Marxism)

Craig Becker

Nominated by President Obama to the National Labor Relations Board (NLRB).

Has ties to SEIU and Blagojevich
http://townhall.com/tipsheet/MicheleBachmann/2009/10/22/obamas_card_check_nominee_hits_road_block

Michelle Malkin says:
> "Perhaps worst of all, Becker has written that the NLRB should be able to enact card check even without Congressional action. Unions could get what they want without Members of Congress having to face the music from their constituents.
> According to the Wall Street Journal (http://online.wsj.com/article/SB10001424052748704107204574471393545371128.html)
> "In a 1993 Minnesota Law Review article, written when he was a UCLA professor, Mr. Becker argued for rewriting current union-election rules in favor of labor. And he suggested the NLRB could do so by regulatory fiat, without a vote in Congress."
> In essence, he'd strip American workers of the secret ballot and Congress would be entirely unaccountable to the American people for doing so!
> If card check passed, intimidation and harassment would run rampant in the workplace when voting to unionize. The right to a secret ballot is as American as it

gets, and to take that privilege away for union gains is simply wrong. The decision about whether to unionize is a serious one and the process should be conducted with safeguards in place."
http://michelebachmann.townhall.com/blog/g/6a54ca44-ac54-4cb8-97fc-4658eb1c5c8e&trackbacks=true#commentAnchor

www.ingramcontent.com/pod-product-compliance
Lightning Source LLC
Chambersburg PA
CBHW021241280526
45784CB00005B/2192